C000185702

WORLD CYCLING STRIPPED BARE

By Sean Conway

www.SeanConway.com

Published by Mortimer Lion Publishing

ISBN: 978-0-9574497-0-1

Cover photo by: Saraya Cortaville
Cover model: Monique Ziervogel

Special thanks to:
Martin & Missy who took care of me in America.
I shall never forget your generosity.

Contents

About Sean

Sean Conway woke up one day, realising he was sick of the rat race, wanted to do something that would shape the rest of his life. With virtually no cycling experience, Sean decided that he would try and become the fastest person to cycle around the world. Six months before he departed he had no bike, no funding and couldn't even cycle 40 miles without having to catch the train home.

Find out everything from equipment, nutrition, training, safety, sponsorship, and how to go from cycling 40 miles to 200 miles a day.

Sean really believes that ANYONE can cycle around the world. The hardest part is getting to the start line. This book will make sure you are as prepared as you'll ever be when you get there.

Foreword

OK! Honestly, how many of you are reading this purely because of the front cover? I don't blame you. Having a naked model on a cyclist definitely is what it says on the tin - 'Cycling the World – Stripped Bare'. There was talk for me to be naked but seriously, no one wants to see that. Although I should have done it anyway to embarrass my future grandchildren. Inappropriate old people are awesome.

So anyway, yes, I have a naked model on my back. I'm not trying to be Richard Branson here or anything, I just really, really, really, believe that ANYONE can cycle around the world. If that means taking one for the team with a risqué front cover to get my point across then that's just what needed to be done. Now that I have your attention, let's rewind to eight months before I set off to cycle around the world.

I was unhappy in my job, my girlfriend dumped me and I had itchy feet. I wasn't in the position to take a gap year after high school and a part of me has always wished I had.

I'd been following many adventure cyclists for years. The likes of Tommy Godwin, Nick Saunders, Alastair Humphreys, Mark Beaumont, Vin Cox and Alan Bate all did some inspirational rides. To me these guys were superhuman and cycling around the world, much like going to the moon, was something that *'other people did'*. I never thought in a million years that I had it in me to do it.

Then one day as I lay in a cold bath waiting for the hot water to rise, I began to think; to dream of what it would be like to cycle around the world.
I thought of all the places I hadn't been to and the list was long: USA, South America, Australia, most of Eastern Europe... the list went on.

As the hot water rose, so did the little fire burning inside of me. I knew nothing about cycling and hadn't cycled for years, but what I did know was that I wasn't happy in my life and felt like I needed to do something about it.

It was then that I decided to go for it. It was the best decision I've ever made. It changed my life. You too can do it. Anyone can do it! All you need to do is say YES!

This is more of a guide than a novel. It details everything from training, the logistics, getting sponsorship and stories from the ride itself. Perfect for toilet or train reading. Or better still, a train toilet.

There is a section at the back for you to write notes. Please do that. I hope to see this book full of underlines, circled words and ideas that will fuel your adventure of a lifetime.

Happy reading . . . and remember to put the lid down when you're done!

Introduction

I couldn't even cycle 40 miles!

Now that I had my mind set on cycling around the world I figured I'd better actually go for a ride. I was fairly fit but I had never cycled more than 60 miles in one day and hadn't been on a bike for about 3 years.

I dusted off my old, spider web covered, oversized bike and decided to try and cycle the 60 mile London to Brighton route. I got up early and hit the road heading south. The weather was good and there was no head wind. Perfect conditions.

I managed through London quite well, even if a bit slow and stopped after 15 miles for breakfast. I felt good! That was until I got back on the bike. My legs started to burn a little. It wasn't too bad though and was to be expected for my first ride.

At around mile 30, I hit the Surrey Hills. In hindsight they were pretty small but at the time I struggled up them, my heart bouncing off the handlebars. I reached the top and lay down in a pool of my own sweat for about 10 minutes convinced that there was less oxygen up here at the top of the hill.

I got back on the bike again and the burn was killing but I was determined to carry on. My progress was short-lived though as I got a puncture 5 miles later. Not to worry though: I had a puncture repair kit. What I hadn't realised was that the glue goes hard if you leave it your bag for 3 years. So there I stood, in the middle of somewhere rural with a flat tire and no way to fix it.

Google Maps to the rescue. I managed to find a bike shop about 5 miles away. Not too bad. It could have been worse. I then spent the next hour and a half pushing my bike along the road while having to dive into the hedgerow every time a truck flew by. I arrived at the shop tired, annoyed and with sore feet. I managed to put a new tube in but in putting the tyre on again with tyre leavers managed to puncture the tube again.

This little 'easy' bike ride was turning into a nightmare. I had been out now for 5 hours. It became clear that I knew nothing about 'proper' cycling.

Eventually I got back on the bike and managed another 10 miles but my legs were totally gone. They had stiffened up from the walk and my knees hurt.

I also forgot to refill my water bottles so was feeling dehydrated. I couldn't go on and found the nearest station and took the train home, depressed at how ignorant and useless I was.

How on Earth was I going to cycle around the world?

What is cycling around the world?

According to Guinness Guidelines, cycling around the world means you have to cycle 18,000 miles passing through two antipodes and generally go east or west.

If you feel this is an important set of guidelines to follow then go ahead. It certainly helps with the route process. If you are going for the world record, then you'll have to follow it.

Some people, including myself, think their guidelines aren't what round the world cycling should be all about. For instance, you could follow their rules and only cycle USA, Australia and a bit in Europe. That's not cycling 'around the world' in my eyes.

For me cycling around the world was to try and do as much as I could (time and budget allowing) in each continent while still following Guinness Guidelines about generally going West.

Some people might want to avoid flying until they reach an ocean. I personally like that idea and if I did it again would try it that way. (Fly as little as possible.)

Also I don't think the total mileage is important. Yes, you need to do enough to warrant it being around the world but zigzagging in one country purely to make up more miles doesn't make it more of an 'around the world' experience.

It's your adventure so do what you feel is right for you. You'll probably only get one chance at it. Make it count!

Getting the ball rolling – Buy a huge world map.
So you've decided to follow in the footsteps of some of the world's most adventurous characters. Carving your own story across the globe will shape the rest of your life. It's a big commitment and failure is NOT an option. It can sometimes be overwhelming but following the right steps and keeping your goals in mind will not only mean success, but also help getting the most of your adventure.

I was amongst nine people all setting off to cycle around the world: five of them gave up for various reasons. You don't want to be one of those failures. Giving up is not an option. Write that down!

Firstly you need to acknowledge why you want to

cycle the world. Maybe you have a desire to see the world? Maybe you want to test your own limits? Maybe you love cycling? Maybe (like someone I know) you want to find a husband/wife? Not the quickest way but I can see how it might work.

Maybe, just maybe, it's as simple as just wanting to have the adventure of a lifetime. There are a million reasons and none are better or worse than the other.

Be honest with yourself and make sure you keep your goals in your mind. It will help you on those dark days. And yes, there will be many!

My aim was to cycle around the world as fast as I could. The world record was one of my objectives but I didn't want to sacrifice adventure for a line in yesterday's newspaper. With this in mind, I decided to do a bit in every major continent. (Not that icy one of course, although that would be incredible.) I also really wanted to raise money for charity. So my reasons were pushing myself way beyond what I thought was possible while trying to help people less fortunate then myself.

It was important for me to have these solid goals as

I could have quite easily given up after I was run over by a pick-up truck doing 50mph in America.

I spent three weeks off the bike with a fractured back, whiplash and concussion, and if I hadn't kept my goals in the front of my mind, I could have quite easily been on a flight home.

Sit down now and write your goals down. Draw them on the ceiling above your bed. (I actually did that. Ask your landlord first though. They tend not to like it.)

Writing them down gets you excited about it, but also keeps your mind focused on making the most of your adventure.

Deciding on a route

This is when the millions of butterflies really start going crazy in your stomach. You are actually going to be cycling, with your own two legs, around the entire planet.

There is nothing more exciting than having a very large world map sprawled out on your kitchen table. So many countries. So many roads. Where do you go?

Time away and when to leave

You also need to decide how long you want to go away for. You can cycle anywhere from 350 – 1200 miles per week. The shorter time you have away the faster you'll need to cycle, but the cheaper it'll be.

Also leaving the UK in February means you need to cycle through Europe in winter, which isn't fun. The short days and cold nights make for pretty slow progress. If you do decide to do that, then I'd be inclined to head as fast as possible down to the South of France where it'll be a lot warmer.

Leaving in July (and going East) means hitting the USA in their winter. In my opinion if you are going to do any winter cycling at all, then do it properly: go to Siberia. That's the only place you need to cycle in winter. Everywhere else is just miserable and you'll have nothing to brag about.

The way around it is to leave the UK in March and head for South America via Spain. That way you get summer almost all the way around. Just some food for thought. Keep researching.

Budget (will talk about sponsorship later)
Your budget will be affected by the countries you are in; whether you stay in hotels or not; how fast you cycle; how long you are on the road and how many flights you take.

You don't have to spend a fortune to follow your dream. Just look at Alastair Humphreys who spent over four years cycling more than 45,000 miles on less than £7000. So it can be done.

Here is roughly what you might need:
Flights: £700 - £3500
Equipment: £1500 - £5000
Misc Visas etc: £500
Money for actual ride: £3000 - £8000

Here are the categories I have worked out. I have gone under the assumption that you are not going to be a beggar and spend 80% of your trip begging for free food. That can sometimes take all the fun out of an adventure. Some may like that, but I prefer to save for a few more months and concentrate on good cycling where I can afford good food.

£5000 – Shoestring with basic gear; a few flights and no hotels.

£10,000 – Longer on the road with more reliable gear; a few flights, an occasional hotel and good food.

£15,000 – Fast with more flights and hotels 75% of the time.

£20,000 – Record attempt; best equipment; restaurant food, hotels most nights and a flight to each continent.

Again these are guidelines. You really can do it a lot cheaper but then be prepared for a lot of low nutrition bread and beans.

How many continents do you want to do?
I wanted to do a bit of every continent, which for me *was* cycling around the world. But that's just me. You might not think that's important which is perfectly fine.

The one problem with going to every continent is the extra flights involved. I hate airports. This also puts a big dent in the budget.

Below are a few pros and cons for each continent.

Europe

Pros - There is no excuse not to cycle in Europe. It is beautiful, very cycle friendly and because the countries are so small you get a whole new experience every few days.

On one occasion I had breakfast in Macedonia, lunch in Kosovo and dinner in Albania. I loved that.

Cons – Can be quite expensive. Not having people to chat with due to language barriers can make solo tours a little lonely.

USA

Pros – I found Americans some of the friendliest people in the world, especially if you're not American. Everyone was so helpful and being able to communicate does help pass the time and understand quick directions from a driver at a traffic light.

The scenery is also varied. America does throw everything it can at you: tornadoes, high mountains and hot deserts, they have it all. It certainly can make your tour a lot more adventurous. Something I actively look for. There are also motels and campgrounds everywhere and are usually not too expensive. It's also safe to cycle at night which means you don't have to stress about getting somewhere after dark. Easy to find spares and food.

Cons – Can be expensive. Some states aren't that cycle friendly.

South America

Pros – Very cheap and the people are friendly. Amazing scenery and it's right up at the top of the adventurous scale.

Cons – Safety is always a worry. I had to get twelve police escorts for the last few days cycling into Lima. This was mainly because I was cycling a lot at night though.

Africa

I haven't done that much cycling in Africa but I was born in Zimbabwe so know what its like.

Pros – Can be cheap. You definitely get the most adventure points by going anywhere near The Sudan. People are generally very friendly too.

Cons – It can also be expensive (for foreigners) and you will be seen as a walking wallet. There is also that constant worry about safety. You'd probably be fine but I wouldn't do any night cycling and would try and sleep somewhere safe. Will be hard to find spares.

Australia

<u>Pros</u> - English speaking and very cycle friendly. You can pretty much camp anywhere. Easy to find spares.

<u>Cons</u> – Very, very expensive. It blew me away. In three weeks I could only afford three nights in a motel. Food is also ridiculously expensive in the Outback. I paid £6 for a 1.5 litre bottle of water. Bonkers! The roads, although good, are very rough and you land up going through tyres very quickly.

Asia

<u>Pros</u> – Cheap everything! Food, hotels, spares, etc. You feel like you are on more of an adventure in Asia. People are very friendly too.

<u>Cons</u> – Roads can be bad and sometimes the constant attention can get annoying. I say just roll with it and have fun. There is no point in fighting it. Many people get ill in Asia and that can add unwanted days or weeks to your tour. Make sure you keep healthy and clean. (Read hygiene

section.)

Which countries are on your target list?

So now that you've decided on continents, you need to think what countries you want to go through.

There are some countries that just won't let you in. Some are really unfriendly toward female cyclist. Some have big hills. Some have lots of dirt roads. Some are really hot and others are really cold. Some are really expensive. All these things need to be considered.

It might not be possible to do every country on your list but no doubt you have a rough idea already. Here is my top 10 to cycle in:

1: Peru
2: Chile
3: Thailand
4: Italy
5: France
6: Great Britain
7: Bosnia.
8: USA.
9: Croatia.

10: India.

I actively look for really adventurous countries to cycle through. That's why places like The Atacama Desert are high up on my list.

Round The World Logistics

Coming up with a route and choosing all the countries you're going to explore is the fun part. It's now down to the logistics. Putting a bit of effort in now can make your tour a whole lot smoother, and can save loads of time.

Visas

First thing you need to do is find out which countries you'll need a Visa for. This can take time and places like the Indian Visa Office in London are about as organised as a pile of dead seaweed!

Honestly! Since they have outsourced the Visas to a private company, logic has all gone out the window. I've had two Indian Visas before (which are in my current passport) yet when I went to get my third one they wanted to send my passport to Ireland (I have an Irish Passport) to verify who I was.

I explained that I am a UK resident and have actually never lived in Ireland. They wanted bills but all my bills in my flat were under my flatmate's name. So basically if you don't have a British passport and don't have any bills in your name (they don't accept mobile phone bills) then you cannot go to India.

Eventually they accepted some old bills from years ago. This whole process took two weeks. The other problem with the Indian Visa was that it's only valid for six months from the day you get it, not the day you enter India. This means if it takes you seven months to get to India you're going to have problems.

America and Australia are two other countries where everyone needs a Visa beforehand and they can be both done online.

Most other countries don't require a Visa beforehand but do make sure you know the deal. Imagine cycling for two months and getting turned away from a border.

Flights
If you have a lot of flights then it might be worth getting an 'around the world' ticket. I used STA Travel and it was great value and they offer a great service. The only problem is that it's almost

impossible to know when you'll be at an airport and I suffered loads of extra expenses to move many of my flights. Pre-booked flights can be a good deal but can also hinder your flexibility. There's nothing worse than meeting some other cyclist and saying you can't join them on an epic route into the Himalayas because you need to catch a flight. I'd definitely look at the options of buying each flight at the airport. It may not be all that more expensive.

Flying with your bike.

This takes years off your life. I'm almost certain the grey patch in my beard only happened after my first flight. They never look after your bike and on one occasion even managed to leave my bike behind.

What you'll need to do is try and find a bike shop in each town you're flying from. Get a box and pack your bike up properly. No cutting corners. Throw in loads of newspaper, plastic, the works. I would also prop my water bottle sideways against both sides of the box, which helped it from getting flattened. I also wrapped my towel around the cross bar for extra protection.

If you have a derailleur then make sure you cover it with a small box. Anything to stop it getting bent. Being a luggage handler is a stressful job and they see millions of bags every month. Yours is just another big heavy box. They will not care for it as much as you would. Fact!

Some say that just a plastic cover for your bike is good enough. The thought behind this is that the baggage guys can see it's a bike and might look after it better. I'm not so sure. I've seen the series of conveyor belts behind the scenes. Your bike will take a bashing. It's not like they'll bring it on a red carpet right to your feet.

Meeting friends and collecting parcels

If you can meet friends around the world then I'd highly recommend it. It's a great motivational booster and nice to share stories with someone you know. Let's not forget, it's also an actual bed. That in itself is worth at least a 100 mile detour.

They'll also know some good places to explore in the area. It is often hard to work it so that you arrive at their home when they are free. It's quite easy to forget that most people have real jobs and can't just drop everything to meet you, even if they really want to.

Try and arrange a rough time when you

leave and then confirm again about three weeks before, if it might change.

The other great thing about meeting friends around the world is you can pre-send parcels of spares to them. I would send a new set of tyres, a new cycle jersey, some recovery shakes, a spare chain and some brake pads. It felt like Christmas and putting on a clean cycle shirt makes you feel like superman, even if only for a day before it gets covered in blood from a nosebleed due to the heat.

Another place that will happily receive parcels are bike shops. I found a few around the world and they were more than happy. In fact, they generally really want to meet you too. Make sure you look into whether the parcel might have import duty. That happened to me in Ecuador and I landed up not getting my package, which had a new clean fresh jersey.

I was gutted and so was the man sitting next to me on the flight out. I did not smell good. Sorry buddy!

Equipment

This section is largely focused on taking the best, most reliable and lightweight equipment I could. My goal was to go with an entire setup of 16kgs.

I may be a little on the 'minimalistic' front but am a huge fan of lightweight touring. Simplifying what you take helps you focus more on cycling and the adventure side of things.

You now have an exciting yet slightly daunting task of getting all the gear needed to take you around the globe. I knew nothing about bikes and the last bike I bought was a deal I found online – DON'T do that, unless you already know the exact bike and size. It landed up being way too big for me.

You need to 'feel' the bike, pick it up, ride it, give it a name. You need to fall in love with your bike. It's very important to adore the bike you are just about to spend the next six months straddling. If you don't then in a moment of anger you might throw it off a cliff. That's a long walk home!

The Bike

I started to look at complete bikes but I either found really fast bikes, which were light but not strong, or really strong bikes that were heavy. It was hard to find a light and strong bike.

I realised that I needed to put one together from scratch. I had never built a bike before. That prospect really excited me. For the first time in my life I'd have full control on every part that made up my bike. Wow! I couldn't wait.

Frame

The first thing to choose is the frame. This will be the base of your bike: the thing that will never change. Your frame is basically your bike so you need to get a good one and I did a lot of research into the various options.

You have four different materials you can choose: Carbon, Aluminium, Titanium or Steel. They each have good and bad points. I could go into lengthy details about how rigidity and flexibility effect energy dispersal but those aspects didn't concern me. What I want to know is: will it break? Can I fix it? Is it comfortable to ride? Does it weight a tonne?

Carbon:

Very light with 'trendy' designs if you're into that. There is nothing wrong with wanting a sexy bike. Remember, you need to fall in love with your bike. The problem with carbon is that if it breaks you are in trouble. It's also so expensive to fix it's not worth the hassle.

Carbon is fairly comfortable but not the best. Also be careful about quality. There are as many cheaply made carbon frames as good ones. Also good carbon frames are really expensive.

Aluminium

Heavier than carbon but a lot stronger and more durable. It often has a worse ride but is a lot cheaper. It's also generally not economical to fix. Aluminium doesn't rust which is a plus point.

Titanium

Generally the same weight as aluminium but can be fixed. Slightly better ride but a little more expensive. One plus point is that it doesn't rust so is better against the elements.

Steel

Steel frames have been around since the dawn of cycling. They are a little heavier than other materials but definitely give the best ride. They do rust however, so you need to watch for scratches in the paint. They can be welded pretty easily anywhere in the world too.

With this I decided to go with a steel frame. A choice I have never regretted.

I looked at many steel frame builders in the UK and finally went with Thorn. They are well known for making high end touring bikes and their Mercury frame with Reynolds 853 tubing seemed just the thing for me. The finished bike weighed in at around 11.5 kgs, which is a lot lighter than my 16kg first touring bike. Not bad for the ride comfort and durability.

While I was cycling across America, a pick up truck drove right into the back of me at 50 mph. I was completely knocked unconscious and suffered a compression fracture to my spine; whiplash; concussion and torn muscles in my leg. It was a pretty serious accident.

If I had a carbon bike it probably would have turned to dust. My steel frame however only took a hit to the rear fork and could have quite easily been bent and welded into working order if I needed to.

Seeing such little damage from such a severe accident truly showed the benefit of having a steel frame for touring.

The other benefit for steel was when flying with your bike. No matter how much you wrap up your bike, somehow luggage handlers still manage to put massive dents and tears in your box. I knew that my frame would take all the sliding and bumps that airports could throw at her.

Wheels

This was a fairly easy choice. I wasn't going with carbon and didn't want to feel like I was driving a tank. I went with some DT Swiss RR 465 wheels, which were a healthy balance between strength and weight and took 700c tyres. They weighed in at 465g for just the rim and cost about £50.

I might have needed slightly stronger wheels if I was heavier or carrying more gear but that's the benefit of lightweight touring. You get to use faster rims. Do your research though. Heavy rims kill your speed and stopping distance.

One morning in The Atacama Desert I got up at 3.20am and hit the road early. I had cycled 174 miles the day before and only had six hours sleep. I was knackered! By now the Pan American was getting a bit patchy in places but wasn't bad enough to warrant cycling slowly.

I was still bombing along at 20 mph but needed to keep really focused on the road to see upcoming holes. This was still early on in my ride so hadn't learned the ins and outs yet.

I needed to see where I was so got my phone out to check my maps. I turned the screen on and it literally blinded me, it was so bright. I turned it away from my face but I still couldn't see a thing as I was bombing along at 20 miles an hour.

I started to brake but it was too late. I hit a series of potholes that actually hurt my wrists. Game over, I thought. There was no way my front wheel survived. I screeched to a halt, my eyes still adjusting.

I got off the bike and was shocked that there was nothing wrong with it. I couldn't believe it.

Lesson 1: Never check your phone while cycling down a hill at night!

Tyres:

This is a big one and really makes a HUGE difference to your speed, stopping distance, and ride quality. Firstly you need to decide on a size.

Most of my route was black top so I could get away with race tyres. I decided against 23c and went with 25c as they are basically the same weight and you get a far better ride on a slightly bigger tyre.

I tried so many tyres in training. From super lightweight race tyres to heavy puncture proof tyres. I met so many people on the road with heavy touring tyres that weigh 900g each and heard the same thing every time: "But I haven't had one puncture."

Guess what. I only got 1 puncture every 500 miles and that included my Peru and India legs where the roads were bad, really bad. All on 200g tyres.

What were they? Continental GP4000s. These tyres are incredible. My last front tyre did 5500 miles and I only got 5 punctures on it. They are fast and puncture resistant.

I haven't found a better tyre to date and at 200g you could carry another four with you and you'd still be lighter than getting one of those heavy puncture proof tyres.

Saying that, if you are going to do a lot of off road sections in your tour then yes, you need to buy a bigger, more durable tyre but if you are going around France for a few weeks and sticking to cycle paths and tarmac roads then there is really no need to get 'tank tyres'.

Gear Systems
This was a tough one too. For me there were only two options really. Standard derailleur or Rohloff hub gear.

Derailleur
99% of all geared bikes in the world have derailleurs. They are easy to find and easy to fix and a lot cheaper. The problem is you *will* probably have to fix and replace them at some point on your tour.

Also you'll need to know how to tune them, but that's not hard. YouTube to the rescue. This is easy to do in France but if you are in the middle of the Atacama Desert, then not so easy.

Also derailleurs don't like flying as they often get knocked or bent in aeroplanes. It's not always possible to get a good bike box when you arrive at an airport. You also need to change your chain and cassette more often as they wear quicker because of all the gear changes.

Rohloff Hub
Expensive! Wait! REALLY EXPENSIVE and if they break, you are pretty screwed. BUT! And it's a big but. They are VERY reliable. There are stories where people have done over 100,000 miles and never even looked at the hub. You also don't have to change your chain as often.

I decided to go with the Rohloff and have never looked back. I never had any problems with it at all. I got a bit of an oil leak during some flights, but this is quite common when leaving the wheel on its side. Other than that I had no problems at all.
It was great not to have to think about it. I just knew that wherever I was going, my hub would work.

All that said:

Although I am a massive fan of Rohloff, I have to admit the price is such a big factor. You need to be doing a seriously big trip to justify the cost.

If you are cycling home through the Sahara and need reliability then go for the Rohloff. If you are going around Europe for a few months, then a derailleur will do you just fine.

Pedals - You have a few options here.

Standard flat pedals

These are great if you want to ride in flip flops/Crocs. Never understood how people can cycle in Crocs but it's a lot more common than you'd think. In The Outback, I met a Japanese guy cycling with five panniers and a trailer, cycling 'the wrong way' around Australia. You have to go anti-clockwise otherwise you will have months, seriously, months of headwinds. He didn't do his research and was only doing 50 miles per day – all wearing Crocs. Fair play to the guy, he was still all smiles.

They are comfortable but very slow as you rely totally on your quad muscles to push the bike forward and often strain your calf muscles and lower back because of the lack of rigidity in the sole.

Flat pedals with toe strap

These are good if you want to cycle in trainers. They allow you to use some of your hamstrings, which means you aren't relying an your quads all the time.

These are probably the most common of touring pedals. The downside for me is not having a rigid sole and sometimes the toe strap can cut into your feet. One benefit is you can wrap some waterproof material – or a plastic bag in my case – around them, which stops spray from getting your feet wet.

Road clip in

The main benefit of clip in pedals is that you can really make the most of all your leg muscles in moving you forward and don't have to rely on just your quads.

Road shoes are the lightest option but you really can't walk in them at all. It's actually quite funny to watch. While stopped for a coffee in Italy, another couple of cyclists came in. Now the waitress at this café looked like she had just come off a shift at Stringfellows. Honestly. Outfit and all. Not at all what I expected from a little mountain café.

Anyway, as these two lads came in, it was hilarious to see them slipping and sliding all over the show (trying to play it cool) in their road shoes as they both wanted to get the counter first. I chuckled to myself quietly. For all I know they saw her last night at Stringfellows.

MTB clip in

You get the benefit of being clipped-in and shoes that you can walk in. For me, this was a no brainer. MTB clip in pedals with Specialized MTB race shoes. The comfort of MTB shoes with the clip in performance advantage was certainly the best option. I could have gone with a slightly more comfortable shoe to walk in but would have sacrificed on performance. Either way you have many variations here.

Just make sure you learn how to clip out of your pedals before going on a ride through London. Falling over at a set of lights in front of a line of cars you've just raced past is up there with telling your mate at school he has a fit mum, not realising she is right behind you. I've done both. Cringe!

My first set of pedals (Shimano XTR) lasted me 12,000 miles. The right pedal started to go somewhere in Malaysia and then one morning, as I was powering through the centre of a town, the pedal came clean off the shaft.

I swerved to the right, nearly running over a pedestrian. "Just my luck." I thought. I stood there for about five minutes trying to bash the pedal back on with a brick, before looking up and right in front of me, all big and bright was the biggest bike shop I had seen for weeks.

I couldn't believe my luck. I went in and bought a pair of £20 Malaysian knock offs. They were good to start with, but after 2000 miles the clicking started. One click every revolution. EVERY REVOLUTION. Click, click, click. Ninety times per minute for 12-15 hours a day. It drove me mad. I managed another 500 miles before getting another set of cheaper Shimanos in Italy.

Brakes

Two options here. Rim or disc. I was a little nervous about going with disk in case they broke in the middle of India. I'd never be able to fix them.

I went with race calliper brakes. Great for the rims and tyres I used, but not so good if I ever want to put bigger tyres on the bike. The one problem I constantly encountered was the rims wearing down. This happened a lot while training in the wet when mud and grit constantly sand down your rims.

I might be inclined to put cable disks on my bike now and work out exactly how to fix them. It's not the lightest option but you could always leave the back calliper on your bike as a back up should all else fail.

Panniers and other cycle bags

It's an age-old tradition to get pannier racks and put a couple of bags on either side of your bike. This system does work and is quite convenient for knowing where you keep things but does slow you down when there is even the slightest of headwinds.

Also somehow you always seem to fill ALL the space you have available. Have less available space and you'll take less crap. Don't ask me how that works.

I decided to have a variety of saddle bags, stuff sacks, frame and handle bar bags that fitted entirely within the shape of the bike, therefore being a lot more aerodynamic. I loved this system. The bike looked great and the handling was way better.

Handle Bar Bag

Here I simply had a 5-litre stuff sack and inside it was my sleeping bag and camping mat. There are many other variations of bags out there but a simple bag hanging below the handlebars is a must.

Make sure you don't have too many heavy items in this bag as it really effects turning performance, especially when weaving your way through traffic in India. You need all the reaction time you can get.

What I didn't have was one of those big bags where you put a map in the top. The reason for this was because I had tri bars which took up that space. (Will talk about mapping and accessories later.)

Frame Bags

I had three bags along my cross bar. It was quite a good setup because each bag had its purpose. I had a small bag in the front on the top, which held my camera, GoPro and voice recorder (for journal entries.)

A slightly larger bag on the top just below the front of the seat held suncream, passport, swiss army knife, small lock and any other things I needed day to day.

A third bar bag hung in the middle of the cross bar. I had all my tools, puncture repair kits, spare inner tubes, spare chain links and tyre levers in this one. It was a triangular bag, which still allowed space for my large water bottles.

Main Bag

My main bag was a large saddlebag. This was initially was just an 8-litre camelback rucksack with the straps cut off that I tied under the seat with bungee cord.

I then found a proper large saddlebag in America from Revelate. They make the best touring bags. Check them out.

In here I kept my cold weather gear, medicine,

camera charger, spare maps etc. You really only need around 10 litre capacity for all your gear.

Make sure you put your valuables, especially your passport, in plastic zip bags. No matter how waterproof your bags are, water somehow gets in somehow.

In Malaysia, my passport got so wet that my Indian Visa got completely smudged. Luckily they let me in eventually but if I had just had a plastic bag, it would have saved me a lot of stress.

Food Bag
Very Important. Having food at hand while on the bike is right up there with carrying toilet paper. The best solution was to cut a 2 litre Coke bottle in half and strap it to the front under the tribars. On average I'd try and carry 2000 kcal of food, which included mixed fruits and nuts, a banana and a few energy bars. It even fitted a foot-long sandwich! That's what I call *fast food*. Ha!

Rucksack's a no go!
Do not wear a rucksack for cycle touring. They add extra weight to your lower back and also don't allow you to cool down properly. Also you never seem to

put the things you took out your rucksack back in the same place you found them. There always seems to be a bulge somewhere that's poking you in the back.

Helmet

ALWAYS WEAR A HELMET!!!!!! Not only will it save your life as it saved mine, but it actually also helps with sunstroke as it stops the suns rays hitting your head.

When I was hit by a pickup truck in America I was flung onto the windscreen. The rear part of my helmet was compressed from 3cm down to a few millimetres. It did it's job.

I know there are stats saying that helmets might not actually save you but surely if there was even the smallest of chance that it *could* help, you'd wear one. You can live with most parts of your body damaged but if your brain gets damaged then that's a whole different story.

I also don't buy the argument that they are uncomfortable. You've bought the wrong helmet. My helmet was so comfortable I often forgot I was wearing it and would eat an entire meal in a restaurant wearing it. And there I thought people were staring at me because of my ridiculous facial hair.

I went with a very lightweight Giro helmet. It came in at around 200g. This helped for those long days when hunched over in tri position. A heavy helmet puts strain on your neck. I could have gone with a slightly more aerodynamic heavier helmet but it's down to your own personal preference. Make sure you don't get one that's too tight though as you might like to wear a cap underneath it. Also if it's too tight, you get brain freeze when smashing it down hills when it's cold and wet.

Saddle

Firstly. If it ain't broke, don't fix it. If you already have a saddle and haven't had problems then DON'T get a new one. If you don't have a saddle yet, then you need to do some research.

When looking for a saddle and are thinking about performance you need to remember that comfort equals speed too. Many people look at weight only and then get saddle sores which affects their speed even more.

The best balance for speed and comfort for

me was a Brooks Swallow Titanium. Yes it's a bit heavier than other race saddles but I never once had any problems.

If you are getting saddle sores, make sure you have the saddle at the right angle. Sometimes a slight shift or tilt can help.

The only time I had problems 'down there' was if I hadn't washed my shirt for a few days and it started raining. I would then get three days' worth of salt washing down into my groin. That is when salt chafe goes to a whole new level. I sometimes had to waste drinking water to wash away the salt.

Water Bottles

Initially I had three bottles. Two 1 litre bottles and a standard 750ml. These were OK but the best system for me in the end was to simply use standard 1.5 litre bottled water bottles and replace the lids with sports drink lids. This means you can carry 3 litres in two or 4.5 litres in three bottles.

Only in places like the Australian Outback or Atacama Desert would you need more than 4.5

litres of water. I didn't want to take a Camelback as this adds quite a lot of extra weight on your lower back and also doesn't let your body cool down properly.

The most water I had to carry was one section in the Outback where I had to carry 6 litres. On that stretch I added two more cages to the front forks. Even then I didn't have enough as I was drinking about 10-litres a day. I had to make a plan. I couldn't carry 10kg of water so asked a few passing cars to take bottles of water 100km ahead and leave them by a roadside signpost. This worked really well even if the water was boiling hot by the time I got it.

Other than extreme situations you can pretty much get by with 3 litres. It's also a bit of a Catch 22 situation, because the more water you carry, the heavier you are, so the slower you go and the more time you are out in the sun, so the more water you need. Research your route and try not to carry more than necessary.

Also don't be shy to ask people. Water is free and generally people like to help. I filled up my bottles from many people out watering their flowers.

It's also a good way of meeting locals. You never know. They might know a better route for you.

Another thing to consider is a bottle cap. You can do without them in dry climates, but as soon as you cycle on wet, muddy roads the mouthpiece can get full of dirt. You can only imagine the type of bacteria that might land up on your lips while cycling through some of the streets in India.

Camping Gear

I really wanted to save as much weight as possible in the camping department. Heavy camping gear could easily weigh upwards of 3kgs and I couldn't afford that.

There were three main things I needed. Sleeping bag, camping mat (I even considered not taking a mat but have tried that before and it is way too cold) and some sort of shelter like tent, bivi or tarp.

Before even looking into any of these things you NEED to research your route and the climate you'll be staying it. I did Lands End to John O'Groats with a -15 sleeping bag, which was completely unnecessary.

I knew I was going to be in summer for most of the way so didn't need a bag below +10 degrees or so.

Sleeping Bag

Research your climate. There is no point in having a -15 sleeping bag in Australia like one Belgian fellow I met. Felt so sorry for the lad. He had just cycled through Mongolia so needed the cold gear and was now suffering in Oz.

I knew I only needed a +10 at the most and after much research I found a Yeti Passion 1 from Germany. It was comfort +15, extreme +1, so knew I'd need to wrap up a few times in the desert but for the most part it would be perfect. It weighed in at less than 300g. Incredibly lightweight.

For the most part, I wasn't too cold. A few times in Australia, I had to wear all my winter cycle gear and that worked a treat. At worst, I could have bought a lightweight silk liner. I would probably do this next time because my sleeping bag could have done with a wash after a few months.

There was a one night in Australia. I had pushed a hilly 170 miles and managed to find a café. I set up camp on the porch and fell fast asleep. At 1 am I was awoken by security, saying I couldn't stay there.

I then had to pack up and moved around the back where I found a dry spot underneath the café. Perfect! I jumped back in my sleeping bag and fell fast asleep. I got up at around 4 am, and looked out my sleeping bag and realised I had shared a sleep spot with a couple of geese. Nice! I've heard they are the best guard dogs. I'm so glad they didn't think I was a threat.

Camping Mat

It was hard to find something that wasn't around 500g until I came across camping frames – like camping matts but have loads of holes in them. I found a Klymit Inertia X Lite. It was 172g and folded down to energy can size. I went with the half length one but I should have gone with the full length one as the bottom of your sleeping bag gets a bit trashed when sleeping on rocky terrain.

Although it looks uncomfortable, it actually wasn't at all. With having 'holes' in the frame means your sleeping bag doesn't flatten out. This keeps the feathers fluffed which keeps you warmer. These frames have the added benefit of being able to go inside your sleeping bag if you like.

Tent

First rule for camping while touring: a tent is only for sleeping or getting out of the rain. I don't get it when people go on a tour and spend from 6 pm till 10 pm in their tent when it's a lovely evening or there is a perfectly good pub down the road.

I like to cycle all day. Sit and meet locals and then, only when I am ready for bed, set up a tent and sleep. You really don't need a large tent. Something small and minimum will do the trick. There are many out there that are under 1kg. It's up to your personal preference really.

I didn't take at tent at all and managed by camping under the stars, under café's, in bus shelters and cheap motels. The only time I had some sort of shelter was in Australia where the dew was quite bad.

I bought some waterproof fabric, put my bike up against a tree and tied the corners to the handlebars and seat. It made a good little shelter. This stopped the dew settling onto my sleeping bag and if put at the right angle, kept the wind off me.

There was one night in Australia where I could have done with a tent though. I arrived in Mount Isa at around 11 pm. All the motels were full, closed or too expensive so I managed to find a park and took shelter behind a bush.

It was the perfect camp spot. Hidden from passers by, sheltered from the wind and nice smooth grass to sleep on. I jumped in my sleeping bag and because it was getting a little cold at night pulled the bag tight so that the hole was about the size of a tennis ball. Everything was nice a snug . . . . until!

At 4 am I was awoken by the loudest noise. I thought the world was ending. I felt water pouring in through the small hole. It can't be raining. Nothing in the forecast suggested rain.

I frantically tried to loosen the cord while trying to squeeze my body out of the small opening. As I got my head out, I realized what had happened. It wasn't raining at all. I had cleverly decided to set up camp about a foot away from one of those sprinklers that pop out the ground. Not one of the fountain style ones either. This one was directed straight at me . . . or actually the bush behind me.

So there I stood. 4 am. Soaking wet and now had a sleeping bag that wouldn't fit into the stuff sack. The only option was for me to get back into the bag and hope the combination of body heat and slight wind would dry me. By 7 am I was dry and could get up and go.

I can laugh now but at the time I was not happy. Not happy at all.

Cooking Equipment

I've cycled with cooking equipment before and after the first few nights, gave up. It was such a mission cooking enough food and then trying to clean your bowls afterwards was too much time taken away from cycling. I prefer to find cold food in supermarkets and then cycle longer. By not taking cooking equipment means you save a lot of time, weight and space.

Clothing

I've said it before and I'll say it again. Research the climate you are going to be cycling in. Then research it again. It makes such a difference if you don't have to carry big heavy jackets around all the time.

I was lucky that most of my route was summer based so could get by with minimal clothing. I went with the bare minimum. Also make sure you buy good quality gear. Round the world cycling puts everything to the test and if it's cheap, you will need to buy it again.

Socks

One pair – Yes, believe it or not, I cycled 16,000 miles and only used one pair of socks. I know what you are thinking, but it really wasn't that bad. I would wash them under a tap or in a river most days and then wrap them around my thigh at night where my body heat would dry them. This system worked for me but realise you might want another pair. There really is no reason for more than two pairs.

Tights

One pair – Unless you fall and tear them then 1 pair will last a long time. You might want to buy a new pair after 8000 miles or so but as long as you wash the salt out of them as much as possible then you'll be fine.

Also don't buy over the shoulder bib tights as I did. I was cycling through the Atacama Desert one cold early morning where I had four layers of clothing on: compression top, jersey, jacket and waterproof. I must have had some dodgy food the night before when all of a sudden I had a little toilet emergency. With bib tights on you can't simply pull them down and go to the loo. So there I was taking off all my clothes just so that I could get my bib tights off my shoulders. All the while trying to find my emergency toilet paper. I very nearly had to buy a new pair of tights that day, and nearly got hyperthermia from having to sit behind a rock half naked.

Shirt

Again you only need one. Shower in it, swim in it, wash it in rivers. You don't need more. Two shirts get just as dirty and then stink out your bags.

Jacket/Waterproof

I took one of each and didn't wear them much as most of my ride was warm. It's all about layers.

Gloves

1 pair fingerless gloves did the job for me. I did buy some cheap standard (not cycling) gloves in Australia when it was cold in the mornings, but got rid of them as soon as it warmed up again.

Neck Warmer

Great to keep your neck or head warm in the cold and also to stop your neck getting sunburned when it's hot.

Other Cycle Clothes

Because I'm practically a vampire (ginger) I needed to cycle with a long sleeve compression top and slip on leg warmers. This not only stopped sunburn but with the sun not hitting your skin directly actually keeps you a bit cooler. Seeing the salt build up also reminded you to eat more electrolytes.

Sunglasses

A must, not only for glare and wind but also for keeping bugs, stones and other flying things out of your eyes. Make sure you have plastic lenses and not glass. Shafts of glass in your eye is not something you want.

Casual Clothes

This is the section where most people fail miserably and land up adding an extra 3 kgs to their set up. I managed with NO, that's right, NO casual clothes for the first three months until Singapore.

I then gave in and bought some lightweight shorts so that I could let my tights dry at night. I didn't take a shirt, flip-flops, jeans or any other 'luxury items'. I realise that this is pretty extreme. I did get some funny looks boarding flights in dirty lycra. If I did it again, I would probably take casual shorts, t-shirt and flip-flops. Only one pair though and nothing more.

Spares and accessories

Inner tubes and puncture repair kits.

I had two inners on bike (obviously) and three spares. I didn't need three spares for most of my trip until I reached India. It was 45 degrees every day and all my patches melted off. Sorry to the lad who spent two hours fixing all my old patches.

In the future, I would keep one of my spare inner tubes for emergencies only. When I got a puncture I generally put a spare inner in and then fixed the punctured one when I reached a hotel or camp spot. Unfortunately I would then camp and it would be too dark to fix the puncture, so left it.

This would happen a few times and before I knew it, I had three spare inners all with punctures. The problem with that is if you get a puncture in the rain, it's almost impossible to repair it properly.

Another lifesaver was taking a lighter. If it is a bit damp then use the lighter to dry the tyre before putting the patch on.

On the subject of patches, I had the self seal ones. They were in the most part good but literally melt off in extreme heat. If you are going to be cycling in very hot conditions then buy the old school glue based ones. They are better, oh and don't be shy to really sand the inners before putting the patch on. Get some good friction on there. The lad in India who fixed mine actually used a metal file.

Spokes

I had three spare spokes for each wheel. I didn't have one spoke break at all. That was partly due to my lightweight set up, but also because I had really high end spokes which I highly recommend.

I met a chap in France who bought a wheel on the cheap and got four spoke breaks in a three-week tour, which landed up costing him more in fixing costs. Not to mention the hassle.

With spokes, the phrase 'buy cheap and buy twice' is very true. I taped the spokes to one of the back forks with duct tape. You can also put them down the seat post but they can rattle around sometimes. Make sure you have the spoke ends too as you can never get old ones off the broken spoke to reuse them. They get rusted on.

Tool

I took an all-in-one Lezyne tool, which included a

chain tool. It worked for me but I may have had a different opinion had I had a chain break on me. Some people say take all your tools individually. You might save some weight that way, but make sure you don't miss one out.

When I bought new pedals in Malaysia they had a different size Allen Key. Luckily I had that size on the tool. It's also harder to lose an entire tool but quite easy to lose one Allen Key when doing repairs in the dark.

Tri Bars and Bar Ends

Tri bars are a must for any bike, in my opinion. I find it the most comfortable way to push out long flat miles. Especially if there is a head wind.

Not only is it comfortable, it also gives you an extra position to take the strain off your wrists and give your back a rest. You can also tie your maps to the top of the tri bars which is always useful.

Once you are used to cycling in tri position, it then frees up your hand for all sorts of activities. You can write some notes, eat a banana and brush your teeth or even, and I know someone who does this, read a book. Don't do that!

Please don't do any of those if you are cycling on a main road. Always be cycle aware!

I reached India at the worst possible time. It was right before monsoon season when temperatures were well into the 40's. The rain hadn't come yet to cool things down and it was really windy due to the monsoon heading up from the South West.

My tri bars were a lifesaver when pushing into 45-degree headwinds, and not just for the obvious aerodynamic benefits. A more upright cycling position meant hot air would have hit my chest straight on which would have increased my body temperature. At least in tri position the hot air flew over me. As long as I kept my head cool with cool water I managed to only get mild heat stroke twice.

You'll notice I had straight handle bars with bar ends. The bar ends are great for pushing up hills when you are out of the saddle. The straight bar grips are great for getting through traffic when you need fingers on the brakes and the Ergo grips really help your wrists.

Lighting and Dynamo

Because I was spending quite a lot of time cycling at night I had to have a good light. I didn't want to have to rely on battery-powered lights so decided to get a dynamo and bought a Supernova E3 dynamo light. It was so bright that cars used to sometimes flash me thinking I was a scooter. I mounted the light on the front right fork. Ideally you want it above the forks but I needed that space for a front bag.

To power the light I used SON Delux Dynamo which has virtually no resistance. Saved me a few times from running over kangaroos in Australia. Seriously. I never knew there were so many. I spoke to a road train driver who reckons he runs over about 20-30 every night. I can believe that because the smell of rotting kangaroo stank me out every few miles.

My rear light was USB chargeable which could also be charged via the dynamo.

Other bits and bobs

A few other things that you might find useful.
Cable ties and small insulation tape - they are always useful to tie things to the bike and also tie your dissembled bike together for the flights. You

can also strap things like spare spoke to your frame.

Swiss Army Knife - that's just a man thing, right!

Small combination cable lock - nothing more than 150g. You only need it for when you run into a supermarket for food or café to go to the loo. Don't carry a big heavy lock. If someone really wants your bike, they will get it. A small lock just deters the chancers.

Two cycle computers - I like to have two computers. One showing daily mileage and one showing total mileage. It's also nice to have a back up in case one breaks.

Sponsorship

Like me, you might have to rely on some sort of financial sponsorship to follow your dream.

There are pros and cons to getting sponsorship. I did a lot of research and spoke to many different people for ideas. I'm not sure whether I got it right or just got lucky, but managed to secure full sponsorship within a month.

The best people to speak to are Polar guys. Those expeditions are really expensive and they tend to have really good proposals.

Before even thinking of sponsorship you need to have a tagline, something unique about your expedition.

For me, it was attempting the world record. For you, it might be raising money for charity. Get your thinking cap on. It's a very competitive world and there are always other people doing more crazy things than you.

There are two types of sponsorship that you can look for.

Equipment Sponsorship

Getting equipment from companies is generally a lot easier than getting money. The cost of giving away a free travel towel is nothing to a big company. Start an equipment list now and get researching.

Also look at other expeditions to find out which companies currently sponsor them. They might like to get involved with you too. A good angle to go for when approaching companies is telling them that you are going to be cycling through some of the harshest climates in the world and using their gear would be the best product test possible.

Some companies, especially if they have never sponsored before, might not have ever thought about it. It's your job to tell them all the benefits they'll get if you take their gear around the world. Tell them you'll blog about it, tweet it, provide them with photos, etc. Ideally you want to try and convince them to use you in their literature too. If they are bragging about you, then that's even better.

Financial Sponsorship

Why will a company give away their hard earned profits to fund what could be seen as someone's *holiday*. That's my first tip. If you want sponsorship, then you need to have another goal than purely having an adventure. Companies might want to associate themselves with you to raise their company's profile; raise money for charity or tick their CSR box.

There are many angles you can come from but my angle was the charity side of things. I did my research and found companies that gave money to charity already.

My proposal was based around the idea that if the company sponsors me from their charity budget then I'd try and match the money they gave me for the charity of their choice. They would then, in essence, get free publicity.

This is very risky because fundraising is a whole new world and can be a hard slog. If you do go down this route, then you need to make them aware that there might be a chance you don't match the figure. Especially if their charity is providing winter blankets for donkeys in Siberia.

That'd be a tough one to raise money for.

Don't let them own you. You want to be working with them and not for them.

My sponsors were uSwitch.com, which is honestly the coolest company in the world. They were young, fresh and enthusiastic and their office is Alice in Wonderland themed. I couldn't have asked for a better partnership.

Do your research and be realistic with what you can and can't offer them. Below is what my proposal looked like. I printed it out and bound it nicely. Presentation is everything. I also wore a suit to the meeting.

Sponsorship Proposal

Below is the exact proposal I sent off to various potential sponsors.

What is it all about?

A global race covering 18,000 miles would be daunting by plane or car, but London-based photographer Sean Conway is preparing to cover this incredible distance by bicycle, when he competes in the 2012 Global Bike Race.

The race, which will start in Greenwich on 18 February 2012 and end approximately five months later, will see elite members of the international cycling community race against each other in a battle to become the Guinness World Record holder for fastest circumnavigation of the globe by bike.

In order to be eligible, contenders must cycle the 18,000 miles in one direction only, and pass two opposite ends of the earth. If Sean wins this race, he will be only the fifth person in history to break the record!

To be in with a chance of beating the record, Sean and his fellow competitors will need to pedal at least 120 miles a day for 150 days.

That's the same as Chris Hoy cycling over 700 laps of the Velodrome, burning up to 10,000 calories each day - the equivalent of 18 large hamburgers.

Sean said: "I would describe myself as a born-adventurer, and when the opportunity arose to take part in something as ambitious as the Global Bike Race, I knew I had to get involved. Although I am not underestimating the enormous physical challenges that lie ahead, I feel enormously excited at the prospect of doing something so incredibly ambitious. Support from as many people as possible will be vital, if I am to be in with a chance of breaking the World Record and I am urging anyone who thinks they can help me in any way - be that through sponsorship or simply advice - to get in touch."

Sean - who originally hails from Zimbabwe and moved to the UK to pursue a career as a professional photographer in 2002 - has so far enlisted the help of a personal trainer and sports nutritionist to ensure he stands the best chance of beating the current world record. He is now seeking corporate sponsorship from a UK-based organisation to help him cover the financial costs of entering the race.

As well as smashing the world record, Sean is also hoping to use the race to generate £25,000 for a chosen charity.

Sean is no stranger to ambitious physical challenges and cycled Lands End to John O'Groats in 2008, as well as climbing Mount Kilimanjaro dressed in a penguin suit earlier this year.

About me:
Name: Sean Anthony Conway.
Age: 30.
Profession: Photographer.
Current City: London, UK.
Life Dream: To summit Mt. Everest and to swim the English Channel.
Ambition after Global Bike Race: To further a career in adventure and hopefully inspire future generations to follow their dreams and get out into

the world!

Born in Zimbabwe and growing up on the banks of the Zambezi River in the heart of the African wilderness is a privilege that I will never forget. Spending most of my childhood building forts, climbing trees and chasing elephants out of the garden, sparked a passion for adventure that will stay with me forever.

My commitment to the race:
I have taken a sabbatical from my career, so can therefore dedicate 100% of my time over the next 8 months to promoting the race and my attempt.
I have a personal trainer and massage therapist that are going to make sure I stay in peak physical condition leading up and throughout the race.
My nutritional therapist has worked with the likes of Richard Branson and is going to teach me to read my body's needs and make sure I eat correctly while in different parts of the world
I hope to raise £25,000 for charity. One of the last record holders managed to raise £100,000, so I whole-heartedly believe I can reach my target!

Previous Achievements:

Summiting Kilimanjaro in a penguin suit.
I actually summited twice as I went back down to get a friend who needed help up the mountain . . . and then back down again.

Cycling solo and unsupported from Land's End to John O'Groats, and then on to the Orkney Islands with nothing but a tent and many, many maps. This made me realise how much I enjoy being out in the world on my bicycle.

Climbed ice covered Ben Nevis solo in the middle of winter. Seven people got air lifted off the mountain that day due to icy conditions.

Trekked to Annapurna base camp in Nepal. The Himalayas had a huge impact on me and my dream is to summit Everest one day.

Competed in the The 130km Duzi Canoe Marathon which included 30km of portage. Canoeing is something I really want to get back into.

Opportunities for Sponsors

This is not just 'Sean on a Bike', and my goal is to work with you to aid you in the following:

Increasing your visibility.

Raising your profile by associating yourselves with my attempt.

Improving employee relations by offering your staff a presentation before and after my race.

Increasing media coverage and meeting your corporate responsibility targets by supporting a good cause while raising money for charity.

I aim to do this in the following ways:

I have a website, Facebook page, Twitter page, Blog and YouTube channel that I will be updating from now right up to and throughout the race itself. I will be blogging and sending video updates throughout the race, which means that people can really get involved with my attempt.

You will be able to follow me at all times via GPS tracking online and see my progress against the other riders. This adds a great competitive element to the race for the public to get involved in.

The Guardian Newspaper has expressed interest in

covering my training in the Health section and my race in the Travel section on my return.

Barcroft Media are interested in selling the photos from my race along with blog entries to all the national newspapers on my return.

I am approaching all the London based newspapers and offering them an exclusive on my story as long as they guarantee exposure and blog feeds to their website etc.

I have already received confirmation that photographers and journalist will attend the start day on the 18th February 2012.

Sponsors will not only gain from my own personal press, but also any press that the race itself attracts and press that the charity gets involved in.

My Lead Sponsor will be able to choose the charity of their choice and I hope to raise £25,000 in donations. This will be done by numerous high street days out while in training all over the country.

I still have 8 more months of networking and promotion to do so I am confident in acquiring many more media and social connections.

Sponsorship Options

Platinum Exclusive - £25,000

Exclusive Lead Sponsor (excluding equipment suppliers who only get small logo under 'Equipment Provided By' section of website.)

Option to have your company in website name.

Exclusive Logo on website as Banner plus on 'Sponsor's Page' + any ad you might like to run.

Exclusive Logo on Blog.

Exclusive Logo on Facebook.

Exclusive Logo on Twitter.

Exclusive Logo on Promo Video.

Exclusive Logo on all Cycling related clothing.

Exclusive Logo on casual clothing (T-Shirts, Fleeces and Track Tops etc) for PR talks and interviews etc.

Exclusive Logo on cycling equipment, including a flag on back of my bike.

Exclusive Logo on all promo material including posters, flyers etc!

I will come and give a presentation to your staff before and after the race about my experience including a slideshow of photos.

I am a photographer and you will receive all photos

taken on my race at high resolution copyright free.

I will provide you with two days of corporate photography to be used by the end of 2012.

I hope to raise £25,000 for the charity of your choice. (I have charities in mind that are 'trendy' right now and would gain more exposure but that is up to you.)

Platinum Non-Exclusive - £20,000

Non-Exclusive shared sponsorship but with main Logo.

Option to have your company in website name.

Main Logo on website as Banner plus on 'Sponsor's Page'.

Main Logo on Blog.

Main Logo on Facebook.

Main Logo on Twitter.

Main Logo on Promo Video.

Main Logo on all Cycling related clothing.

Main Logo on casual clothing (T-Shirts, Fleeces and Track Tops etc) for PR talks and interviews etc.

Main Logo on cycling equipment, including a flag on back of my bike.

Main Logo on all promo material including posters, flyers etc!

I will come and give a presentation to your staff before and after the race about my experience.

I am a photographer and you will receive all photos taken on my race at high resolution copyright free but shared with other sponsors too.

I will provide you with 1 day of corporate photography to be used by the end of 2012.

I hope to raise £25,000 for the charity of your choice. (I have charities in mind that are 'trendy' right now and would gain more exposure but that is up to you.)

Gold - £15,000
Non-Exclusive shared sponsorship but with smaller main logo than Platinum.

Main Smaller Logo on website as Banner plus on 'Sponsor's Page'.

Main Smaller Logo on Blog.

Main Smaller Logo on Facebook.

Main Smaller Logo on Twitter.

Main Smaller Logo on Promo Video.

Main Smaller Logo on all Cycling related clothing.

Main Smaller Logo on casual clothing (T-Shirts, Fleeces and Track Tops etc) for PR talks and interviews etc.

Main Smaller Logo on cycling equipment including a flag on back of my bike.

Main Smaller Logo on all promo material including posters, flyers etc!

I will come and give a presentation to your staff before and after the race about my experience.

I am a photographer and you will receive all photos taken on my race at high resolution copyright free but shared with other sponsors too.

I hope to raise £25,000 for the charity of your choice. (I have charities in mind that are 'trendy' right now and would gain more exposure but that is up to you.)

Silver - £10,000

Non-Exclusive shared sponsorship.

Shared Logo on website on 'Sponsor's Page'.

Shared Logo on Blog.

Shared Logo on Facebook.

Shared Logo on Twitter.

Shared Logo on Promo Video.

Shared Logo on all Cycling related clothing.

Shared Logo on casual clothing (T-Shirts, Fleeces and Track Tops etc) for PR talks and interviews etc.

Shared Logo on cycling equipment, including a flag

on back of my bike.

Shared Logo on all promo material including posters, flyers etc!

I will come and give a presentation to your staff after the race about my experience.

I am a photographer and you will receive all photos taken on my race at high resolution copyright free but shared with other sponsors too.

Bronze - £5,000

Non-Exclusive shared sponsorship.

Shared Logo on website on 'Sponsor's Page'.

Shared Logo on Blog.

Shared Logo on Facebook.

Shared Logo on Twitter.

Shared Logo on Promo Video.

Shared Logo on all Cycling related clothing.

Shared Logo on casual clothing (T-Shirts, Fleeces and Track Tops etc) for PR talks and interviews etc.

Shared Logo on cycling equipment, including a flag on back of my bike.

Shared Logo on all promo material including posters, flyers etc!

Copper - £1,000

Non-Exclusive shared sponsorship.

Shared Logo on website on 'Sponsor's Page'.

Shared Logo on Promo Video.

Rusty Nails - £500

Shared Logo on website on 'Sponsor's Page'.

The Actual Ride

Mapping

There are many cycle specific GPS systems out there, which are good for first world countries but not so good for 'off the beaten track' countries. They are great if you want to document your route and look at stats etc, but the downsides are battery life and they are sometimes hard to read in the sun and too bright to read at night.

I am a big fan of actual maps. You can write on them. Makes a good memento when you get home. When I cycled Santiago to Lima, I bought various maps, which I then cut up to make a long thin map for the entire coastal route. There is no point in carrying parts of the map that you don't need.

The only time I had no map was in the USA as it's not practical to get a map for each state. Here I used Google Maps to get by. I also bought an Android phone that would save all Google Maps viewed onto the phone's memory. This meant I didn't have to use 3G all the time.

This system was so good, I managed to use

pre-downloaded maps to get me all the way from Singapore to London. Every time I had WiFi, I would scroll and view the route for the next few days and that would then be saved to the phone.

The GPS 'blue arrow' doesn't rely on reception and aligns to the downloaded map whether you have 3G or not. This helped a lot when navigating through cities where my paper map wasn't detailed enough.

Camping versus Motels

If you can camp, then do it. If you can do it in the wild and away from an actual campsite, then even better.

I used to love the challenge of trying to find a place to camp. It was a little harder for me as I didn't have a tent so places like under cafes, bus stops and farm barns were a real treat when I could find them.

I'd definitely take a sub 1kg tent next time. As I said before, tents are for sleeping and getting out of the rain. I see no point sitting for hours in a tent when there are so many places to see and people to meet.

If it's not raining, then I prefer sleeping with

the tent door open or even under the stars. This way I can keep an eye on my bike (which I've tied to the tent.) I also like to keep a small travel towel in the tent so that I can wipe away the condensation in the morning. You can then use the now damp towel to wipe your face. It's all about multi tasking!

There will be times when camping is not recommended. Especially in parts of Asia near big cities. You can find really cheap motels in those parts of the world and it's sometimes nice to do a proper clothes wash and have a shower.

It also allows you to leave your belongings and do some exploring. Most of the time they'll let you take your bike into the room. I was quite adamant about that.

Rabat in Morocco was the worst place for this. For some reason even the dingiest of hotels wouldn't let me in. I arrived into town at around 10 pm after doing a hard 196 miles. All I wanted to do was have a shower and fall asleep. It took me another hour and *six* hotels later before I found one that would let me take my bike in the room.

I may have had a slight sense of humour failure that evening.

Safety

Keeping safe on the road is very, very important. Being run over can ruin your dream, as it very nearly did mine. It's all common sense but here are things you need to be thinking about.

Reflective clothing - Do it! It makes such a difference.

Reflective tape - Sometimes when it's warm you might not wear reflective jackets. At least then put some reflective tape on the back forks and on the back of your helmet.

Lights – You should have a dynamo front light which is great but also make sure you have a tail light. I used a USB chargeable one which I could charge from the dynamo.

Helmet – You're an idiot if you don't wear one! WEAR A HELMET!

Mirrors – They make the world of difference and are a must for any cycle adventure, especially when you are in tri position. It's hard to look over your shoulder when hunched over.

There were many occasions when I'd need to avoid something (mainly dead kangaroos) and a quick glance down told me whether there was a road train behind me. You can get really small mirrors from Zefal that fold away nicely. I used one each side. One for when cycling normally and the other angled better for when I was in tri position. You should be checking your mirrors constantly but there is one time when you should ALWAYS check them. That's whenever you see an oncoming car. You are at your most vulnerable when you have an oncoming car and an overtaking car passing you at the same time. That's when things get a bit tight.

You need to be very conscious. If it's a road that has no hard shoulder then don't be shy to move into the road a little so the overtaking cars HAVE to slow down and wait for the right time to pass as opposed to trying to squeeze past and pushing you off the road.

Music – When in slight urban or busy areas, then only use one headphone. Ideally you should only ever use one but when you're in the middle of the Atacama and only pass one truck every hour then it's fine to use both.

Look drivers in the eye and smile – if they know that you've seen them then you become a 'real person' and not just a random road obstacle.

Look a bit unsteady – It sounds mad but if you see a cyclist that looks a bit unsteady on their wheels, you will give them more room. Much like how you give a child more room. I would often do a little fake unsteady swerve when cars were about 50m back. They would then give *way* more room.

Keeping Sane

Keeping sane can be tough, especially on those long hot days in the middle of the Outback with no one to talk to except your mascot.

That's my first tip. Take a mascot. Mine was the Little Flying Cow that I bought for £1 from a charity shop in 2008. He has been everywhere with me ever since and stays on my handlebars. We have a great time together. He also becomes the focus for a great set of photographs.

Music can also help make those long hard days fly by. Music really helped me when there was a huge headwind. For some reason, if I couldn't hear the barrage of wind passing my ears then I didn't think it was as bad as it actually was.

Cover your cycle computer. Seriously. When you are having a tough day, then seeing your pathetically slow pace and mileage makes you even more depressed. You could turn them off but I like to record the mileage I do every day.

Eating properly gives you more energy to carry on. There were many times when I thought I was having a bad day, but I was just in fact massively malnourished. Getting the right carbs, proteins and fat can turn a killer hill into a breeze. It's almost impossible to eat too much so eat, eat, eat. The early Race Across America guys used to follow a See Food Diet. If you see food, eat it!

Documenting your tour

Documenting any tour is very important. Even if it's just to prove to your grandkids that you were once cool. Nick Saunders who rode 13,000 miles in seventy eight days in the 80's gave me the best piece of advice. He told me that records get broken or forgotten but having photos, videos and blogs will inspire more people for a lot longer than a line in yesterday's newspaper.

From the outset, I wanted to document my ride as much as I could. As much as you think you'll remember, you won't.

Documenting your tour properly can easily be done with any smart phone. There are so many apps that allow you to update Facebook, Twitter, Blogs and videos. I see so many guys carrying a huge laptop around trying to update their blog, then their battery dies and they can't find a plug point and their adapter is right at the bottom of their bag. Some of them are clever and have a solar charger the size of China that never seems to have enough charge. You don't need it.

A phone is small, light and can be charged from your dynamo.

Another tip is to take a small voice recorder. (Only if your phone doesn't have one.) Unless you are really good at writing exactly how you felt and what you did, then a voice recorder is a great way of documenting everything. It's great listening back to your entries too. You get a real feel for how you felt due to the tone in your voice. They make for some good audio blog entries too.

I also had a GoPro video camera and a

small point and shoot camera with a 15x optical zoom. It's nice to have that option. I also did some video on my phone which I could upload straight to YouTube. It's always nice for people to see videos while you are on route. Makes it more personal.

Online Tracking

Letting people know where you are is another great way to tell your story. You'd be surprised how much help I got along the way from people looking at my website, seeing where I was and then sending me some tips about the area as they had been there before. Twice I even had friends of friends come and find me, which was brilliant.

It's also great to know that your family knows where you are. It can be tough for them, especially if they don't know where you are in the world. Just make sure you change the batteries often as you might stress some people out if your tracker suddenly stops moving for 48 hours because the battery has died.

I used a SPOT tracker that sent a waypoint to my website every 10 minutes. It cost about £130 for the tracker and then £100 per year for the subscription.

Keeping things charged

Keeping cameras, phones, iPods etc. charged is an obvious necessity. It was hard to find one but eventually found a Biologic Reecharge battery kit that could be charged by the dynamo. It had a USB output which allowed me to charge all my gear. I had to also find the USB charger for my camera's battery.

The system was great. It would charge my phone in a few hours and I could charge things even while using the front light although the light didn't shine as bright. The only problem I had was when building my bike in Singapore airport, I accidentally got the cable pinched in the headset which then ended my charging abilities. It took a few days to find some tools to fix it.

I also mounted the battery unit on the top side of the bottom frame. This stopped it getting covered in mud. It seems pretty waterproof as long as you keep the cables plugged in.

Keeping Healthy

Getting ill on a tour is the worst thing that can happen, actually the second worst: getting run over is the worst. Nevertheless, it's not great when you have to spend a week in bed or talking to the big porcelain telephone. Getting ill in third world countries is even worse.

There are a few tips to help you get by:
Take hand sanitizer. Make sure you use it before every meal. Also make sure you sterilize your handlebar grips. They can be full of bacteria and need to be cleaned.

In places like India have a Coke with every meal. Coke has some acid in it, which can help kill off some belly bugs. It's not going to get rid of E-coli but might stop the smaller ones.
Keeping warm – Sometimes when you are pushing long miles, your body struggles to both supply energy to your muscles and keep your core warm. Make sure on the cold mornings you wrap up and eat, eat, eat.

Food gives you the energy your body needs to warm you up. Also don't forget to get your fair share of fruit and veg. It's all too easy to just eat carb and protein for energy. You still need vitamins, electrolytes and antioxidants.

Hygiene

Make the most of rivers, swimming pools and beach showers. I took a small towel which also helps wipe down the condensation on the inside of your tent. You can then wipe you face with it. Baby wipes and a toothbrush are all you need. I didn't even have toothpaste half the time but I wasn't socializing much, so will forgive you if you take a small tube. You might want a small roll-on deodorant but you really don't need anything more than that.

First aid

There are some bits and bobs not to miss.

Antibiotics

There are times when you might feel a bit of flu or a tummy bug coming. Take some antibiotic that you can take just as a clean out. If I felt something coming, I'd take three tablets for one day only. Don't take antibiotics too often as your body can become immune to them.

Imodium

You don't want Delhi Belly. It's not much fun and

can waste time. Imodium is really good and only takes one tablet.

Painkillers

Sometimes after a long hilly day, your knees can take a beating. Having an anti-inflammatory painkiller can reduce the swelling, which allows better blood flow to heal your tendons.

Malaria

If you are going into a malaria area and are camping then do take precaution. Malaria is not something to play with and will probably end your tour if you get it. I suggest a lightweight mosquito net if you plan on camping wild and don't have a tent. I had to abandon camping in Venice due to all the mosquitos. They were pretty aggressive there. Honestly, not even my compression top stopped them from biting me.

Advanced training and nutrition

This section is courtesy of Steve Mellor, my trainer.

Now that you've got a rough idea of the exciting places, and killer hills you want to conquer, its time to knuckle down and do some training. I'm taking it that you aren't a lazy slob and only going to push out 40 miles per day. I think somewhere around 100 miles per day is more than achievable while still being able to enjoy yourself.

Many people say that you can start with no training and get the fitness along the way. This is true but you risk injury and the whole experience is a lot better when you are fit and healthy.

You also really learn a lot about your body the more miles you do. You want to hit that start line the fittest you have ever been, knowing exactly what you're capable of.

I will go over all the aspects that I think will help you have a better, more enjoyable and injury free tour. I'm going on the assumption that you have at least six months to train.

In this section you will read things that touch on all aspects of training, program writing, nutrition and more. There are lots of topics that will require some Googling and further research; things like the exercise plan, to some of you this will be a completely new addition to your weekly routine.

If this is the case, my advice is to read, read some more, watch some YouTube videos and consult an expert that knows a bit about what you're undertaking.

The key to success initially is making the training fun, enjoyable and something you look forward to.

Its also very important that you're not in a rush to get to the 100 mile mark, that will come with time, right now you need to go riding with friends, go spinning or cycle to and from work.

The key is getting on the bike and turning your legs over regularly, get used to what it feels like to go up a hill; down a hill; into a headwind; cope with a cross wind; understand what a "good road" feels like and what a pot holed riddled track is like. But most of all get out and enjoy it: on a weekend try roping in some mates and pick a great lunch spot, then cycle there and enjoy the whole experience.

Before you start training.

Make sure you get a cycle computer for your bike. You need to know what mileage you are doing. It's important to see your progress improve. Monitor both your average speed and total mileage.

Some people like using a heart rate monitor. I don't use one but it can be great way to see the kind of effort you are putting out.

You must remember - recovery is just as important as training. If you don't give your body time and fuel to recover, then you actually become a worse athlete and not a better one.

Stretching strategy – warm up and warm down

Warming up and down is key to not getting injured, it's also a great time for you to learn about your body, and importantly, what stretches work for certain muscles as this is something you will need during each and every day of your challenge.

Key areas for cyclists are: calves, hamstrings, quads (including hip flexors), glutes and lower back. Your upper body will also get tight and tired but the main focus will be the lower half of the body.

Warm up/Cool down

Jump on the bike and get the legs turning for the first ten minutes, stretching is only useful once the muscle temperature is increased, at that point hop off the bike and stretch the lower body out including calves, hamstrings, quads (including hip flexors), glutes and lower back. Hold each stretch for 20-30 seconds repeating each stretch at least twice.

Use YouTube to find the best stretches that work for you; give different ones a go until you're happy with your routine. This routine should be repeated at the end of the ride to help stretch out those muscles you have been repeatedly using each time you push and pull on the pedals. Stretches should be held for 30-40 seconds and each stretch done at least three times or until you feel comfortable again.

6 Months To Go (have end goal i.e. 200miles in two days)

Mileage makes champions. My trainer Steve tells me that all the time and there is a lot to be said for it.

To start with just get miles in the legs. Don't stress about hill reps, time trials or gym work. Cycle for the enjoyment. You may or may not have your 'Round The World' bike yet (read equipment section first before buying) but just use any bike.

I just bought a £50 bike on eBay and it did the job. The key to success here is getting the bike set up properly, do some research into bike set up and the different components of cycling set up.

Then have a look at what you can adjust on your bike and get to work. One crucial aspect is seat height: you want about a 15 degree bend in the back of the knee when your leg is fully extended at the bottom of the pedal revolution. This is something that everyone can get right from day one!

Start cycling to work. Do a few weekend rides but don't push it too much. That comes later. I'd try and do about 100 miles per week. That's all.

Get used to cycling for a while, have a break, eat some food and then get back on the bike. Your legs will be stiff but at least you are learning how your body copes with the sort of strategy that will be used throughout your challenge.

It's an interesting feeling when you get on the bike; learning what works for you to 'get going' again is crucial to your success.

Try to break 100 miles in one day, it's a great psychological boost to get over that milestone and it's a great way to chart your progress.

Last two weeks: See physio for a body MOT! They tell you what's weak and what causes injury. Tell them your training up to now and give them a run down of what you intend to do over the next few months. They need to give you a number of areas to work on so that when you pay them a visit in 4-6 weeks they can see the improvement. This may cost you in the region of £30-70 per hour, however, it will pay dividends to your training and end goal.

4-1 months to go – writing a plan!
Now it's time to start an official routine, from now until the day you leave. After getting used to cycling the key to success is consistency. Consistency is what makes you fitter, stronger, faster and most importantly more robust. Regardless of merit or how good the program is, is WRITE A PLAN AND KEEP TO A PLAN (or as best as you can).

If you're ill, then you rest; if you're travelling, working late, getting agro from your other half, then you do as best as you can. But the best thing to do is make a plan and follow it.

Writing it down means you naturally make it progressively harder, and therefore get fitter rather than jumping in at the deep end or never actually improving. The plan can be written as simply and plainly as you like, as only you have to understand it, you can have all sort of graphs, data, analysis or just simply a calendar with some mileages written on the different days following the guidelines of: Week 1 – easy. Week 2 – harder. Week 3 – hardest. Week 4 – easy, (but harder than week 1) and so on.

That's way better than just deciding on a whim each week what to do. It also means it'll be specific. Also be realistic with the time you have. The worse thing is writing a plan you don't stick to. It's bad for motivation and can cause you to stop the plan altogether.

It's great to meet your targets each week and has a hugely positive effect on your motivation. Having boxes to tick means you know when you do them and can really see a progression. It takes the questioning out of 'what to do today' as you don't need to think.

Also use advice from your physio and implement

the exercises into your weekly schedule: don't be one of those people that goes to the physio and never does the exercises; it's a waste of your time and money!

Cycling

Should be doing 12-20 hours of cycling a week. This gets progressively more and more each week, but make sure it's achievable though as some of you won't have the time to do 20 hours cycling in a busy week.

Gym

This is there to make you stronger and more robust, NOT BIGGER! It helps to be stronger as well as fitter, the focus is lower/full body sessions. This should be done under supervision of a gym instructor or PT unless you are a competent lifter and know your way around a gym.

Exercises:
Month 1: 3 sets of 10 reps
Month 2: 4 sets of 6 reps
Month 3: 3 sets of 5 reps
Month 4: 4 sets of 4 reps

N.B. for all exercises the weight should increase week to week (even by as little as 1.25kg). For tricep dips and pull ups – progress until you can complete the full reps lifting your body weight and then start to use a weight belt to add additional weight.

Squats (using a barbell) – focus on pushing from both legs (use a mirror in front of you to check form). Keep the back straight and get the ATG (ass to ground), this way you strengthen the glutes as well as the quads.

Lunge (using dumb bells) – either walking or alternate legs, keep the shoulders in line with the hips, lower the back knee down to the ground and push up from the front leg. Slow and controlled is key.

Hamstring curl (seated or lying, this can also be switched to a stiff leg deadlift for the more advanced lifter) – focus on working the hamstring through the full range of the exercise, reduce the weight rather than compromise the range of movement.

Tricep dips – important to strengthen the triceps and shoulders for all the mileage out on the bike. Slowly lower the body down until the shoulders are level with the elbows and push straight back up. Repeat.

Pull ups (because Rocky does them and he's cool) – they're also a great way to strengthen the back and core.

Yoga, Pilates and stretching.
Muscles shorten being in one position all the time, hence cyclists are constantly picking up niggles, aches and pains that they live with day-to-day. Going to a weekly yoga/pilates/stretching session will help to prevent and teach you how to manage your aches and pains. Do it. Keep flexible. More likely to do yoga in the plan rather than do your own stretching.

3 & 2 months to go – Re-evaluate last month's session. Make changes if needed, making sure it's still realistic. The plan you made a few months ago might now be completely 'out of date' because goals, objectives, jobs, or home life may have changed.

This is a good time to reflect and make any amendments.

Final Month – Taper! Especially in the final two weeks you need to chill out; give the body a break; focus on getting the body in the best RESTED state possible.

Time to go for a few massages and any time spent on the bike should be at a maximum of two hours. No need for anymore at this point. Fitness, on a physiological level, takes time. By this I mean, if you go out training then your body is not instantly fitter, it takes roughly 7 - 21 days to gain that fitness, as your body need to make lots of adaptations that take time.

So if you're training in the two week lead up to your start date then that training will be completely nullified by the time it comes to churning out 100+ miles per day.

Take the time to relax and get fired up. If you're going out of your mind thinking you're losing fitness then jump on the bike and get out there but just know that this is not PHYSIOLOGICALLY recommended, however if it helps you

PYSCHOLOGICALLY then go for it.

The Do's

Follow a plan, your plan, don't be afraid to amend the plan.

Talk to as many experts as possible and do the following:

Get your bike set up properly.

See a physio early on.

Show someone your training plan.

Tell all your friends about it and try to get them out on rides in the early days.

Learn the routine that works for you when getting back on the bike after a lunch break.

Embrace yoga/stretching, DON'T neglect it.

The Don'ts

Don't read loads of forums and change what you are doing every week, do lots of research and make decisions.

If you miss a session, don't feel you need to make it up.

It's a six month program. Not one day. If you miss many sessions, re-evaluate the program.

Nutrition

Have you been buying the same food for the last five years. I know I have.

Things to get right.
First Rule! Eat enough! Make sure you get the calories in. Your stomach wont be big enough to start with. You might feel full but not have had enough food to sustain the effort you are putting out. Start looking at the nutritional information on everything you buy.

Nutrition is something that is quite often overlooked. I knew nothing about nutrition when I cycled around Britain and it made things a lot harder than they could have been.

You get two types of people. People who live to eat and people who eat to live. Some people will sacrifice maximising nutrition for flavour and experience; and some people, like myself, just eat whatever is needed for maximum performance.

Either way you will need to eat certain things. Make sure you eat properly while training and on your ride. You need to get the necessary protein and carbohydrates in order to recover efficiently.

I would have protein shakes before and after every ride, containing roughly 100g carbs and 15g protein. If you don't have the correct recovery, then your body won't heal your muscles properly and the next time you ride you won't be as strong.
Better recovery = better performance!

As I said before the most important thing for you is: GET THE KCALS IN. If you are low on kcals, then it doesn't matter how much carbs, protein and fat you're eating at what time and in what quantity.

The golden rule is to work out the figure you intend to expend while riding, add another 500 kcals on top; if you lose weight over a period of a week then add more kcals on top. If you gain weight, then cut some kcals down - simple!

Once you have the total kcals nailed down, start to look at the breakdown of food: aim for 50% fat, up to 1.8g/kg of body weight from protein and the remainder is your carbs. Again this is simple, although you may need to dig out a calculator to do the sums!

Carbohydrates (CHO):
You may have experience in this department. You've heard the phrase carb-loading. Carbohydrates are a source of energy.

What are CHO and what are they used for?
CHO are an energy source for high intensity exercise, essentially any sugar (including fruit) is a CHO. Meaning any CHO is sugar, therefore, pasta/ potatoes/ rice/ bread are all made up of sugar. This sugar is stored in the body as glycogen and when glycogen stores are full, it gets stored as fat. **CHO should be used in your diet to help you train harder, faster, stronger and recover quicker.**

Things that are true:
CHO can improve performance.
CHO can be ingested as a liquid or solid.
To optimise recovery consume CHO at 0.5 g/kg body weight – 1.5 g/kg body weight immediately after intense training sessions.
Hi GI CHO are the best kind of CHO to eat immediately after training to maximise recovery.

Low GI CHO are the best source of CHO to eat - *except* immediately after training.

Things that are false:
If you're hungry then CHO are the best things to snack on as they fill you up.
CHO are essential for every training session. Fat is better.
Carb loading doesn't work.
You should drink Lucozade in every training session.
Pasta is a good meal to have in the evening when not training.
Your CHO stores are completely empty when you first wake up.
You should always eat CHO at breakfast. Fat is good too.

Things that are misunderstood:
CHO should make up 60% of all athletes diets
You should have 7-11 servings of CHO everyday
You need to eat pasta, rice or potatoes with every meal
If I eat CHO they will always make me fat.
I don't need to eat any CHO after training because I

am trying to lose weight.

Carbs are an interesting one and during your training they are important to maximise recovery and fuelling.

However, one of the great training adaptations you can make during your training is to become a better fat burner; the reason being that out on the roads, this is your main energy source.

What you eat can affect this, so you need to stop stuffing your face full of carbs and start to think about fat as your main source of energy. 1g of carbohydrates = 4kcal, 1g of fat = 9kcal, meaning you have to eat half as much fat to get the same amount of energy: or more applicably, you have to carry twice as many carbs to get the same amount of energy as you would from fat.

Protein:
Your muscles need protein to build and heal.

What are proteins and what are they used for?
Proteins are used to build and repair muscle. They are also responsible for making hormones and enzymes which help you to exercise harder, quicker

and recover better. They can be found in meat, beans, cheese, milk, yoghurt, nuts and more.

Things that are true:
Protein improves recovery from training sessions.
Protein should be consumed at 0.8 g/kg – 2.5 g/kg depending on the sport. (Roughly 1.4g/kg BW – 1.8 g/kg BW for touring cyclist)
Protein should change as training demands change.
Protein should be consumed immediately after training (inc. cycling sessions.)
Protein can be consumed in a shake to maximise the speed it can be consumed after training and absorption into the body.
More protein doesn't always equal increase muscle mass.

Things that are false:
"Protein shakes are bad and are full of illegal substances" - you should get all of your protein from food.
"I don't do any weight training so I don't need any protein."
Protein from plants is the same as protein from

meat.

You don't need to eat protein because your body can make it.

Things that are misunderstood:

"Eating too much protein is bad for your liver" – not true, an unproven myth in all except for those who suffer from gall stones.

If you want to build lean muscle mass then you just need to eat loads of protein.

Eating too much protein will make me increase body fat.

Protein is an essential part of your diet, the key is knowing how much and when. When you cycle your body will burn off some of the protein stored in a 'free pool of protein' within your body, the longer you ride the more is burned off. Hence the more you ride, the more protein required.

Having protein immediately after cycling or training is crucial to help alleviate tired and sore muscles while also promoting training adaptations to occur within those muscles. Going 'light' on protein can equal rapid weight loss and high feelings of fatigue.

Fat:

Better for you as has twice as much energy as carbs.

What are fats and what are they used for?

Most people think FAT is bad, this INCORRECT! Fat should be your friend! Fat is essential for life; it is crucial for hormonal production and is used as an energy source throughout the day when effort levels are high. However, eating CHO switches off fat burning. Remember that it can take you body weeks to turn on the fat burning process so start eating fat NOW.

When I cycled through Croatia I met Polish Paul and we cycled for 4 days together. Three times Polish body-building champion and now endurance cyclist Paul, took the fat burning to a whole new level.

His daily diet was:

Breakfast

5 egg Omelette (Protein) with 15 small hotel style bars of butter (fat)
Some figs (carbs) and cheese (fat and protein)

During the ride

On a 120 mile (200km) ride all he would eat/drink is full fat cream, 30% if possible and it worked. He was strong and had loads of energy. 200ml of 30% cream is nearly 700kcal. Have two of those and you get 1400kcal in about 2 minutes.

Post ride

He'd have some pasta and meat for recovery. It was really interesting watching him. I personally think he needed more protein near the end of the day but he managed on mostly fat and didn't crash at all.

That's quite extreme but it's proof that fat can work if you get your body conditioned to burning it.

Things that are true:
There are good fats and bad fats; good fats are the naturally occurring fats found in dairy and meat. Bad fats are manufactured fats, found in man made foods and oils e.g. processed meals/meat, vegetable oil, etc.
Fats are essential for life – for hormonal production, energy, growth, enzyme activity, transport of other

molecules.
Full fat is good.
Low fat is bad.

Things that are false:
Skimmed milk is better as it has low fat content.
You shouldn't eat more than four eggs a week due to the cholesterol.
Cholesterol is bad.
Low fat is good.
Full fat is bad.

Things that are misunderstood:
Fat makes you FAT – this is a massively INCORRECT statement. Naturally occurring fats, including saturated fat, do not make you fat!
All athletes should eat low fat diets.
Low fat diets will reduce body fat and is the best method to use when trying to reduce body fat.
Cheese is bad and you shouldn't eat it.

So this one may take some time to get your head around; do some reading into fat and it's importance to athletes.
Take a look at the Paleo way of eating and

research why the 'fat is bad' slogan is not true. In terms of your cycling challenge, the first key focus is getting the kcals in.

I know there is a lot to get your head around and to be honest there is a whole book in itself just on nutrition. What I wanted to do was just let you know about what worked for me, and some info that you might like to go off and research yourself.

Happy eating!

Coming home

It's so easy to get so involved in your adventure you probably won't think at all about what you do when you get back. You might have a job waiting for you but if you don't, then there are a few things you should think about.

Coming back to normal life is tough. Really tough. It's well documented that people fall massively a few weeks after getting back. Think about it. You've spent six months of your life with a purpose, a goal, following your dream, seeing new places and experiencing new things. You've now done it. You succeeded and had the time of your life. Now what?

Your body has also gotten quite used to having high levels of endorphins in it and your mind has been constantly bombarded with new challenges, hard times and problem solving. You're now in a one bedroom flat, it's raining and the only dilemma you have is whether to have tea or coffee with breakfast. No matter how strong you are, you will struggle. Everyone does.

I am currently in that situation. Not being one for the old 9-5 means that getting a job I hate purely to exist is against all my morals. I've decided that doing some writing is a great way of not only cementing my memories but is a great way to look back on a great adventure. Even if you don't publish it, write it down anyway. Your grandkids will love it someday.

Also schools love to hear stories, so go in and tell them about your adventure. It's a great way of reliving the journey as well as inspiring a generation.

Conclusion

My cycle around the world was the experience of a lifetime and was the best decision I've ever made. Although my dream of the world record was demolished by a reckless driver in America, I still managed to refocus my other goals, push myself way beyond what I *ever* thought possible and complete 16,000 miles in 116 days.

I may not be the fastest person to cycle around the world but I certainly had one of the biggest adventures of my life. I am certain that had I not researched all the different aspects detailed in this guide properly I'd have probably not finished.
The hardest part is getting to the start line. Once you are there then everything falls into place.

So there you have it. Everything you need to cycle around the world. If I can do it, then so can you. Please let me know if this has inspired you to do a big cycle ride. I'd love to hear your stories.

Sean Conway

Round the world in figures

Miles cycled: About 16000 (Cycle computer broke so just guessing)
I am short on what I wanted to cycle but my accident meant I was on the road a month longer than expected and needed to get back to London for the Olympics

Bike Make: Thorn Mercury frame with Rohloff Hub

Bikes used: 2
First frame got completely mashed in accident and was generously given another one by the wonderful family that took me in in Arkansas.

Pedals: 3 sets
My first XTR pair lasted 12000 miles then came off the shaft. 2nd pair (Cheap Malaysian knockoff) lasted 2000miles.

Tyres: 14
I mostly used Continental GP4000s tyres which are incredible. My last front tyre did 5000miles and I only got 5 punctures on it. (Back tyre wears quicker) I posted tyres to bike shops/friends around the world which I would collect along route.

Punctures: Around 40
I didn't get that many punctures and many of my flats (especially in India) were old patches melting

off. I would take proper glue based patches next time and not self stick ones.

Food and water consumed:
I would eat and drink my entire body weight every week to 10 days. On average I would drink 8 litres per day and up to 12 litres on the heavy 40+ degree days.
Most water carried at one time: 6 litres

Weight lost: 5kg
I didn't have much to lose as I was only 67kgs to start but went down to about 62kgs in Malaysia.

Clothing worn
Tights: 2 pairs (First pair got cut off me in hospital)
Gloves: 3 pairs
Socks: 1 pair (This pair also did Lands End to JOG)
Jacket and Waterproof: 1 set
Shoes: 1 Pair (S-Works MTB. Love these shoes)

The Accident
Speed at which truck hit me: 50mph
Speed I was travelling: 10mph
Time of accident: 5.56am
Time completely unconscious: 10 minutes
First words spoken when awoken: "How's my bike?" (I'm not making that up either)
Injuries sustained: Whiplash. Concussion. Torn ligament in right leg (Cant squat now).
Compression fracture to T11 vertebrae. Torn muscles in the middle of my back. Sprained ankle.

Chipped tooth.
Hospital bill: $15,000
Time for injuries to heal: Still not healed.
Time spent off the bike due to injury: 25 days
Distance cycled before injury: 4000 miles
Distance cycled with injury: 12000 miles

Average hours spent on bike
Pre Accident: 16 hours per day
Post Accident: 12 hours per day
Shortest Day: 7 hours
Longest Day: 21 hours

Average Hours Slept
Pre Accident: 5-6 hours
Post Accident: 7-8 hours

Average Cycle Distances
Pre accident: 180 miles per day
Post accident: 140 miles per day
Days cycled less than 100 miles: 6
Days Cycled over 180 miles: 20
Shortest Day: 78 miles
Longest Day: 226 miles
Average Speed: 13.5mph
Longest distance cycled without available food/water: 190 miles

Days cycled in rain: 15
Pretty happy about that. I planned my route to be summer based.

Hottest temperature cycled in: 44 degrees
Days cycled that were over 30 degrees: 75
Times I got heatstroke: 4
Nose bleeds due to heat: 5

Road kill count: 32346789876543 (Mostly
Kangaroos in Oz)
Chased by dogs: Around 50 times
Bitten by dog: Once

Times I fell over: Once (At ferry in France on
second to last day in front of a huge crowd)

Chains used: 4
I would try and get a new chain every 4000 miles or
so.

Times I shaved: 0

Notes

World Cycling Stripped Bare

World Cycling Stripped Bare

World Cycling Stripped Bare

World Cycling Stripped Bare

_____

_____

_____

_____

_____

_____

_____

_____

_____

_____

_____

_____

_____

_____

_____

_____

_____

_____

_____

_____

_____

_____

_____

_____

_____

If you've managed to fill in all these pages then you are ready. Go now and have the adventure of a lifetime.

CPSIA information can be obtained at www.ICGtesting.com
Printed in the USA
LVOW07s0802220815

451155LV00032B/1145/P